Lyrics/Poetry & Drama Inspired by the Holy Bible & Life's Experiences

by

Malisha Deonta Harris

RoseDog Books

PITTSBURGH, PENNSYLVANIA 152222

ISBN: 978-1-4349-9439-4
Printed in the United States of America

First Printing

For more information or to order additional books, please contact:
RoseDog Books
701 Smithfield Street
Pittsburgh, Pennsylvania 15222
U.S.A.
1-800-834-1803
www.rosedogbookstore.com

Acknowledgements

First, I would love to give the Father, the Son, and the Holy Spirit all the honor and glory for being my strength throughout my entire life.

To my family and friends: Thanks for listening to me talk and express myself when I was a little girl. I appreciate you all and each person is truly dear to my heart.

Love with the Love of Christ Jesus, Always,

Malisha

(Or Scooter-Tab, as my Grandpa Ed would call me when I was a little girl. In memory of him for encouraging me to accomplish all the dreams and visions God places in my heart and mind to make each dream and vision come true in my lifetime.)

Contents

Lyrical Writings

God knows your every desire
He knows your pains
God knows your sorrows
He knows your joys

Just keep him near you
He'll never leave
Just seek him my child

11 November 2001

Glory—Glory
Repeat x 3
Glory to God's name

Reach out your hands
And let him in
God loves you

Glory—Glory
Glory to his Holy name

Give God thee Honor
Give him the Praise
Reach out your hands
And place them in his

God will take care of all your needs
Give him all thee Honor
Give him all the Praise

Glory—Glory
Repeat x 3

Reach out your hands
Let him in
Give God all your problems
Leave them be

Entrust your faith in God
Glory—Glory
Repeat x 3

06 December 2001/revised 21 December 2001

By the Blood of Jesus
We are washed
We are clean
We are saved
We are healed
We are loved
We are free

By the Blood of Jesus
We have protection
We have strength
We have power
We have peace
We have joy
We have eternal life

By the Blood of Jesus

16 June 2002

Glory, Hallelujah!
God's grace and mercies
Shine upon me
Shine upon me

Hallelujah, God Almighty!
Your wisdom and your power
Shine upon me
Please shine upon me

18 June 2002

I need you all around

I need you everyday
           Every hour
           Every minute
           Every second

I need you, Lord,
All around me

In the morning
In the noonday
at night
In the midnight hour

I need you, Lord,
All around me

20 June 2002

I wake up in the morning
The sun kisses my face
I say dear Lord Jesus
I thank you
Today

I wake up in the morning
The sun kisses my face
I say dear Lord Jesus
I give you all your praise

I wake up in the morning
The sun kisses my face
I say dear Lord Jesus
Send me on my way

I wake up in the morning
The sun kisses my face
I say dear Lord Jesus
Bless me today

I wake up in the morning
The sun kisses my face
I say dear Lord Jesus
Let me .
Bless someone
Today

20 October 2002

Direct me
Guide me
Lead me in the direction
You would have me to go

Dear Lord…

1 July 2002

You must believe in Christ
To have eternal life

There is no other
Like Jesus Christ Our Lord

You must believe in him
To have eternal life

Jesus Christ
Jesus Christ
Jesus Christ

26 June 2002

True

I gotta be true, Lord
I gotta be true
Help me be true, Lord
Help me be true
Keep my mind on you, Lord
Keep my mind on you
Help me be true to you, Lord
Help me be true
I will stay true to you, Lord
I will stay true to you.

27 June 2002

Heal

Heal me, oh Lord
Heal me today
Keep me, oh Lord
Keep me today
Shine your Light, Lord
Shine it my way
Guide me, oh Lord
Don't let me stray

Lead me, oh Lord
Lead me today
Heal me, oh Lord
Heal me today
Hold me, oh Lord
Don't let me go

Shield me, oh Lord
Shield me today
Love me, oh Lord
Love me today
Touch me, oh Lord
Touch me today
Love me, oh Lord
Don't let me stray

27 June 2002

I call out your name
Giving you all the Praise and Honor
You are my Spiritual Father
I call out your name

Jesus Christ
Jesus Christ
Jesus Christ, Our Lord
And Saviour
I call out your name

29 June 2002

I'm gonna be happy through all of my trials
I'm gonna be happy through all of my pains
I'm gonna be happy through all of my struggles
I'm gonna be happy no matter what…

8 August 2002

Dear Lord

Draw me close, dear Lord
Keep me in your arms
Never let me go

My heart is open to you
My life I give to you

Ever breath I take
I need you
Ever step I make
I need you

Draw me close, dear Lord
Keep me in your arms
Never let me go

11 November 02

Heavy Hearts

I Kneel on my knees for those with heavy hearts
I lift their names to you, God
I pray for their heavy hearts
I pray they give it to you
So you can lighten their heavy hearts
I pray they open their hearts to God
Letting you save their lives
I pray their heavy hearts are free
No longer in captivity
I pray you free each of them with heavy hearts
I pray you teach them the way

For we are your children
By the blood of Jesus
We are free
Our sins are washed away
We are clean and white as snow
Jesus was that Lamb that shed his blood

I give you the praise, the honor,
And all of the glory.
I lift up my hands
And ask
That you have mercy on all the
People with heavy hearts.

I lift up my hands
And give you all of the praise
I am thankful to have you in my life,
Dear Lord
I love you

24 June 2002

The Plays

Ruth ("I'll Go With")

Characters:
Ruth (A Moabite)
Naomi) Mara means "bitter")
Orpah (A Moabite)
Boaz
The Harvesters
Foreman
The Man
The Ten Witnesses
Narrator I
Narrator II
Narrator III
Narrator IV

The purpose of this play is to show how three people remained strong in character and true to God even when the society around them was collapsing.

References: The Holy Bible in the King James Version by Thomas Nelson, Inc. (1984 and 1977); Life Application Study Bible by Tyndale Charitable Trust (1996)

ACT I

Narrator I:	Dark time in Israel's History when people lived to please themselves, not God. [Judges 17:6] Ruth was a destitute widow. Destitute means: in absolute want/need; devoid (of); penniless; broken, distressed, down and out, etc. Join us as we share the story of Ruth one of the women's book of the bible. The most important scripture from this book is "Your people will be my people, and your God will be my God" (Ruth 1:16) Elimelech moves his family to Moab. Elimelech was Naomi's husband. They had two sons. The two sons married Moabite women. Naomi's sons' names were Mahlon and Kilion. Ten years past left Naomi without her sons and without her husband. The setting, Naomi heard in Moab that the Lord had blessed his people in Judah by giving them good crops again.
Naomi:	Go back to your mother's homes instead of coming with me. And may the Lord reward you for your kindness to your husbands and me. May the Lord bless you with the security of another marriage. [All ladies are in mourning dressed in black.]
Narrator I:	Then she kissed them goodbye. and they all broke down and wept. [Crying and weeping tearful expression with deep compassion for one another.]
Ruth and Orpah:	[together] No! We want to go with you to your people.
Naomi:	[with a curious expression with puzzled look] Why should you go with me? Can I still give birth to other sons who could grow up to be your husbands? No, my daughters [with feeling and compassion and concern for their welfare and well being] return to your parents' home, for I am much too old to marry again. [Silence; pause for a moment] And even if it was possible, I was to get

married tonight and bare sons, then what? Would you wait for them to grow up and refuse to marry someone else? [With love] No, of course not, my daughters! Things are far more bitter for me than for you, because the Lord himself has caused me to suffer. [Again together they wept—Orpah as it is her choice to; kisses her mother-in-law good-bye. With love, devotion, dedication, the most important sacrifice took place. Ruth took a chance not knowing the outcome but willing to step up to the challenge. By having faith and stepping out on the unknown with love and respect for Naomi and her God.]

Ruth: [with persistent and determination] Don't ask me to leave you and turn back now. I will go wherever you go and live wherever you live. Your people will be my people, and your God will be my God. I will die where you die and will be buried there. May the Lord punish me severely if I allow anything but death to separate us!

Narrator: Ruth had a burning desire in her heart and soul. The Holy Ghost was placed in her to be a seed for God to allow God to help her grow in him to do his will. Ruth says, I'll go with.

**Play a song here: "It's Alright (Send Me)" by Winans Phase
The children present the Mega Themes**

Faithfulness—Kindness—Integrity—Protection—Prosperity/Blessings

Names of God
Elohim
Yahweh
El Elyon

ACT II

Narrator II:	Meanwhile, they arrived in Bethlehem and Naomi told everyone to call her Mara.
Naomi:	Don't call me Naomi. Instead call me Mara for the Almighty has made life very bitter for me. I went away full, but the Lord has caused me to suffer and Almighty has sent such tragedy. Later, Ruth gleans in Boaz's field. Gleans means: Pick up, gather, and pick up after reapers in grain fields. Now there was a wealthy and influential man in Bethlehem named Boaz, who was a relative of Naomi's husband, Elimelech [all by who you know/associated with very important]. One day Ruth said to Naomi...
Ruth:	Let me go out into the fields to gather leftover grain behind anyone who will let me do it.
Naomi:	All right, my daughter, go for it.
Narrator II:	So Ruth went to gather grain behind the harvesters. Lord and behold, as it turns out, she found herself working in a field that belonged to Boaz, the relative of her father-in-law, Elimelech. While she was there Boaz arrived from Bethlehem and greeted the harvesters.
Boaz:	[Yelling out to the harvesters] The Lord be with you!
The Harvesters:	[replied] The Lord bless you, sir.
Narrator II:	Then, Boaz asked his foreman...
Foreman:	[responded] She is the young Moabite woman who came back with Naomi. She asked me this morning if she could gather grain behind the harvesters. She has been hard at work ever since, except for a few minutes. Rest over there in the shelter.

Narrator II:	Boaz goes over to Ruth.
Boaz:	Listen, my daughter. Stay right here with us when you gather grain; don't go to any other fields. He gently touched her hand, looking into her eyes. [Ruth is bashful, with her head down and avoiding eye contact] See which part of the field they are harvesting, the follow them. I have warned the young men not to bother you. And when you are thirsty, help yourself to the water they have drawn from the well.
Ruth:	[on her knees at his feet, in a soft sweet voice] Thank you kind sir. Why are you being so kind to me? I am only a Foreigner.
Boaz:	Yes, I know all about your love and kindness you have shown your mother-in-law since the death of your husband. I have heard how you left your father and mother and your own land to live here among strangers. May the Lord, the God of Israel, be with you.
Ruth:	I hope I continue to please you, sir. You have comforted me by speaking so kindly to me, even though I am not worthy as your workers are.
Narrator II:	At lunchtime Boaz called to her…
Boaz:	Come and join us and help yourself to some of our food. You may dip your bread in the wine if you like [act of sharing].
Narrator II:	So Ruth sat with them and Boaz gave her food, more than she could eat. She went back to work. Boaz ordered his young men to drop grains on purpose for Ruth.
Boaz:	Let her gather grain right among the sheaves without stopping her. And pull out heads of barley from the bundles and drop them on purpose for

her. Let her pick them up, and don't give her a hard time.

Narrator II: So Ruth gathered barley all day. When she beat out the grain that evening, it came to about half a bushel. She took it to Naomi. Ruth also gave her the food that was left over from her lunch.

Naomi: [looking surprised and excited] So much!' Where did you gather all this grain today? Where did you work? May the Lord bless the one who helped you! [At this time, Naomi was coming out her bitterness.]

Ruth: The man I worked with today is named Boaz.

Naomi: May the Lord bless him for expressing his love and kindness to us. This man is our closest relative, one of our family's redeemers.

Ruth: What's more, Boaz even told me to come back and stay with his harvesters until the entire harvest is completed.

Naomi: This is terrific! Do as you are told. Stay with him and his harvesters.

Narrator II: Ruth continued to work alongside the women in Boaz's fields and gathered grain with them, too. But all the while she lived with her mother-in-law.

Names of God
El Roi
EL Shaddai
Yahweh Yireh
Yahweh Nissi

ACT III

Narrator III: Ruth follows Naomi's plan. Take it from Ruth; she did not mind taking direction, guidance, or orders from the authority people in her life, Naomi and Boaz.

Naomi: My daughter, it's time that I found you a permanent home, so you will be provided for. Boaz is a close relative of ours, and he's been extremely kind by letting you gather grain with his workers. Tonight he will be winnowing barley at the threshing floor. Now do as I tell you—take a bath and put on perfume and dress in your nicest clothes. Then go to the threshing floor, but don't let Boaz see you until he has finished his meal. Be sure to be notice where he lies down; then go and uncover his feet and lie down there. He will tell you what to do.

Ruth: I will do everything you say.

Narrator III: So she followed the directions and guidance exactly and completely. That evening after Boaz had finished his meal and was in good spirits, he lay down beside the heap of grain and went to sleep. Then, Ruth came quietly, uncovered his feet, and lay down. Around midnight, Boaz suddenly woke up and turned over. He was surprised to find a woman lying at his feet.

Boaz: Who are you?

Ruth: [With soft voice] I am your servant, Ruth. Spread the corner of your covering over me for you are my family redeemer.

Boaz: The Lord bless you, my daughter. You are showing more family loyalty now than ever by not running after a younger man, whether rich or poor.

[Touched her head] Now don't worry about a thing, my daughter. I will do what is necessary, for everyone will know that you are an honorable woman. But there is one problem. While it is true that I am one of your family redeemers, there is another man who is more closely related to you than I am. Stay here tonight and in the morning I will talk to him. To see if he is willing to redeem you, then let him marry you. But if he is not willing, then as surely as the Lord lives, I will marry you! Now lie down here until morning.

Narrator III: Ruth lay at his feet. When morning arrived, Ruth left.

Boaz: [Before light hit] No one must know that a woman was here at the threshing floor. Bring your cloak and spread it out.

Narrator IV: He measured out six scoops of barley into the cloak and helped her put it on her back. Then, Boaz returned to the town.

Naomi: So what happened, my daughter, Ruth?

Ruth: He gave me these six scoops of barley and said don't go back to your mother-in-law empty-handed.

Naomi: Just be patient, my daughter, until we hear what happens. The man won't rest until he has followed through on this. He will settle it today. [Naomi paced back and forth.]

Play a song: **"My Redeemer Lives" by Reuben Morgan**

Names of God
Adonai
Yahweh Elohe
Yisrael
Yahweh Shalom
Qedosh Yisrael

ACT IV

Narrator IV: Boaz went to the town gate and took a seat. When the family redeemer came, by Boaz called out to him.

Boaz: Come over here, friend. I want to talk to you. [They sat together. Boaz called ten leaders from the town and asked them to sit as witnesses.] You know Naomi, who came back from Moab. She is selling the land that belonged to our relative Elimelech. I felt that I should speak to you about it so that you can redeem it if you wish. [Boaz is demonstrating an act of consideration for his fellow man, offering him Ruth even though he desired that Ruth be his wife.] If you want the land, then buy it here in the presence of these witnesses. But if you don't want it, let me know right away because I am next in line to redeem it after you.

The Man: All right, I'll redeem it.

Boaz: Of course, your purchase of the land from Naomi requires that you marry Ruth, the Moabite widow. That way, she can have children who will carry on her husband's name and keep the land in the family.

The Man: Then I can't redeem it, because this might endanger my own estate. You redeem the land; I cannot do it.

Narrator IV: Back then, in those days the custom in Israel for anyone transferring a right of purchase to remove his scandal and hand it to the other party. This was a public validated transaction. So Boaz redeemed the land.

Boaz: You are witnesses today that I bought from Naomi all the property of Elimelech, Kilion, and Mahlon. And with the land I have acquired Ruth, the Moabite widow of Mahlon, to be my wife.

Ten Witnesses: We are witnesses! May you be great in Ephrathah and famous in Bethlehem. (Ruth 4:11-12)

Narrator: So Boaz and Ruth marry and bear a child called Obed. Ruth's faithfulness and obedience lead her life with a legacy that was significant even though she couldn't see all the results.

Names of God
Yahweh Sabaoth
El Olam
Yahweh Tsidkenu
Yahweh Shammah
Attiq Yomin

Esther ("Beauty Is Greater Than Skin Deep!")

Characters:
Esther [Hadassah(means Beautiful); A Jew]
King Xerxes I
Haman (The enemy)
Mordecai (A Jew)
Zeresh (Haman's wife)
Queen Vashti (A woman who stood up for her principles regardless of the consequence. Was she right in doing so? If you were her, would you have done the same?)
Mehuman, Biztha, Harbona, Bigtha, Abagtha, Zethar, Carcas [The seven eunuchs: castrated man, especially one formerly employed in a harem]
The Seven Officials
The Attendant(s)
Hegai (An eunuch/An agent for the king)
Narrator I
Narrator II
Narrator III

The purpose of this book of the Bible is to demonstrate God's sovereignty and his loving care for his people. Main Verse: "If you keep quiet at a time like this, deliverance for the Jews will arise from some other place, but you and your relatives will die. What's more, who can say but that you have been elevated to the palace for just such a time as this?" (Esther 4:14)

References: The Holy Bible in the King James Version by Thomas Nelson, Inc. (1984 and 1977); Life Application Study Bible by Tyndale Charitable Trust (1996)

ACT I

Narrator I: Esther becomes queen; The King's Banquet. See Esther 1:1-9 to narrate.

King Xerxes: [Half drunk] Bring me Queen Vashti—Mehuman, Biztha, Harbona, Bigtha, Abagtha, Zethar, and Carcas.

The Seven Eunuchs: [Went and came back] Queen Vashti refused to come, your Majesty.

Narrator I: The King was furious and burned with anger. He immediately consulted with his advisers, Carshena, Shethar, Admatha, Tarshish, Meres, Marsena, and Memucan—seven high officials of Persia and Media.

King: What must be done to Queen Vashti? What penalty does the law provide for a queen who refuses to obey the king's orders, properly sent through my eunuchs.

Memucan: Queen Vashti has wronged not only your Majesty but also every official and citizen throughout your empire. Women everywhere will begin to despise their husbands when they learn that Queen Vashti has refused to appear before your majesty. She must be banished from your presence, and you must choose another queen more worthy than she. When this decree is published throughout you vast empire, husbands everywhere, whatever their rank, will receive proper respect from their wives.

Narrator I: King Xerxes and his princes agreed with Memucan's counsel. Meanwhile Xerxes' anger had cooled. He decided to start his search for a new queen.

King: Let us search the empire to find beautiful young virgins for the king.

Narrator I: The king appoints agents in each province to bring these beautiful young women into the royal harem at Susa. Hegai will see the ladies are all given beauty treatments.

Hegai: Your Majesty, after that, the young woman who pleases you the most will be made queen instead of Vashti.

Narrator I: The king made the plan effective immediately. See Esther 2:5-9 to narrate. [God's Anointing falling upon Esther] Meanwhile Mordecai was demonstrating his loyalty to the king. He over heard Bigthana and Teresh trying to assassinate the king. Mordecai passed this information to Esther.

Mordecai: Esther, two of the king's eunuchs are planning to kill the king. They are Bigthana and Teresh.

Esther: I will tell the king of this, Mordecai.

Narrator I: When an investigation was made and Mordecai's story was found to be true, the two men were hanged on a gallows. This was all duly recorded in the Book of the History of King Xerxes' Reign. Later, Haman's plot against the Jews and Haman's promoted and Mordecai refused to bow down or show respect.

Palace Officials: Why are you disobeying the king's command? [Day after day this question was asked.]

Narrator I: Word gets back to Haman. He saw that Mordecai would not bow and he is filled with rage. Haman learned that Mordecai was a Jew. The Jews only service one God and bow only to their God. This is when Haman decided to destroy all the Jews throughout the entire Empire of Xerxes. See Esther 3:7 to narrate.

Haman: There is a certain race of people scattered through all the provinces of your empire. Their laws are different from those of any other nation, and they refuse to obey even the laws of the king. So it is not in the king's interest to let them live. If it please your majesty, issue a decree that they be destroyed, and I will give 375 tons of silver to the government administrators so they can put it into the royal treasury."

Narrator I: See Esther 3:10 to narrated.

King: Keep the money, but go ahead and do as you like with these people.

Narrator I: See Esther 3:12-15 to narrate.

Children present the Mega Themes
God's Sovereignty, Racial Hatred, Deliverance, Action, Wisdom
Play a Song: "Every Season" by Nichole Nordeman

ACT II

Narrator II:	Mordecai requested Esther's help. See Esther 4:12 to narrate.
Mordecai:	[Reply back to Esther] Don't think for a moment that you will escape there in the palace when all other Jews are killed. If you keep quiet at a time like this, deliverance for the Jews will arise from some other place, but you and your relatives will die. What's more, who can say but that you have been elevated to the palace for just such a time as this?
Esther:	Go and gather all the Jews of Susa and fast for me. Do not eat or drink for three days, night or day. My maids and I will do the same. And then, though it is against the king, if I must die, I am willing to die.
Narrator II:	So Mordecai went away and did as Esther told him. Three days passed when Esther put on her royal robes and entered the inner court of the palace. The king welcomes Esther.
King:	What do you want, Queen Esther? What is your request? I will give it to you, even if it is half the kingdom!
Queen Esther:	If it pleases Your Majesty, let the king and Haman come today to my banquet prepared for the king.
King:	Tell Haman to come quickly to a banquet, as Esther has requested.
Narrator II:	So the king and Haman went to Esther's banquet.
King:	[As they were drinking wine.] Now tell me what you really want. What is your request? I will give you whatever you desire, even half the kingdom!

Esther: This is my request and deepest wish. If Your Majesty is pleased with me and wants to grant my request, please come with Haman tomorrow to the banquet I will prepare for you. Then tomorrow I will explain what this is all about.

Narrator II: Haman's plan to kill Mordecai Haman made him happy when he left the banquet. But when he saw Mordecai sitting at the gate, not standing up or trembling nervously before him, he was furious. See Esther 5:9-11 to narrate.

Haman: [Speaks to his wife] And that's not all! Queen Esther invited only me and the king himself to the banquet she prepared for us. And she has invited me to dine with her and the king again tomorrow. [Slightly confused and frustrated.] But all this is meaningless as long as I see Mordecai the Jew just sitting there at the palace gate.

Zeresh: Set up a gallows that stands seventy-five feet tall and in the morning asks the king to hang Mordecai on it. When this is done, you can go on your merry way to the banquet with the king.

Narrator II: This advice pleased Haman, and he ordered the gallows set up. [The king honors Mordecai.] The king had trouble sleeping and ordered an attendant to bring the historical records of his kingdom so they could be read to him. The king discovered he had not rewarded or gave recognition for what Mordecai did for him.

The Attendant: Nothing has been done.

King: Who is that in the courtyard?

Narrator II: Haman had just arrived in the outer court of the palace to ask the king to hang Mordecai from the gallows he had prepared.

The Attendant: Haman is out there.

King: Bring him in. [So Haman came in.]

King: What should I do to honor a man who truly pleases me?

Haman: [Thinking of himself] Whom would the king wish to honor more than me? If the king wishes to honor someone, he should bring out one of the king's own royal robes, as well as the king's own horse with a royal emblem on its head. Instruct one of the king's most noble princes to dress the man in the king's robe and to lead him.

King: Excellent. Hurry and get the robe and my horse and do just as you have said for Mordecai the Jew, who sits at the gate of the palace. Do not fail to carry out everything you have suggested.

Narrator II: [Haman eating his words.] Zeresh and all his friends warned Haman and suggested to him to stop opposing Mordecai. While they were still talking, the King's eunuchs arrived to take Haman to the banquet Esther had prepared. [Haman's execution.]

King: [While they were drinking] Tell me what you want, my Queen. What you desire is yours, Queen Esther. I will give you half the kingdom.

Queen Esther: If Your Majesty is pleased with me and wants to grant my request, my petition is that my life and the lives of my people will be spared. For my people and I have been sold to those who would kill, slaughter, and annihilate us. [Meanwhile Haman is getting nervous and anxious.] If we had only been sold as slaves, I could remain quiet, for that would have been a matter too trivial to warrant disturbing the king.

King: Who would do such a thing? Who would dare touch you?

Esther: This wicked Haman is our enemy!

Narrator II: Haman grew pale with fright before the king and queen. Then the king jumped to his feet in a rage and went out into the palace garden. But Haman stayed behind to plead for his life with Queen Esther, for he knew that he was doomed.

King: Will he even assault the queen right here in the palace, before my very eyes!

Narrator II: The king roared with anger. And as soon as the king spoke his attendants covered Haman's face, signaling his doom.

Harbona: Haman has set up a gallows that stands seventy-five feet tall in his own courtyard. He intended to use it for Mordecai, the man who saved Your Majesty from assassination.

King: Then hang Haman at once!

Play a song: "God of Wonders" by Stacie Orrico

ACT III

Narrator III:	A decree to help the Jews is formed. The Victory of the Jews. The Festival of Purim. The greatness of Xerxes and Mordecai. See Esther 8:1-4.
Queen Esther:	If Your Majesty is pleased with me and if he thinks it is right, send out a decree reversing Haman's orders to destroy the Jews throughout all the provinces of the king. For how can I endure to see my people and my family slaughtered and destroyed?
King:	I have given Esther the estate of Haman, and he has been hanged on the gallows, because he tried to destroy the Jews. Now go ahead and seal it with the king's signet ring. But remember that whatever is written in the king's name and sealed with his ring can never be revoked.
Narrator III:	See Esther 8:9-9:11
King:	The Jews have killed five hundred people in the fortress of Susa alone and also Haman's ten sons. If they have done that here, what has happen in the rest of the provinces? But now, what more do you desire and it shall be granted to you.
Esther:	If it please Your Majesty, give the Jews in Susa permission to do again tomorrow as they have done today, and have the bodies of Haman's ten sons hung from the gallows.
King:	Yes, I agreed Queen Esther, it is granted to you.
Narrator III:	See Esther 9:16-10:3.

"Children Dance Off of Battlefield" by Norman Huthins

Ideas and thoughts on what to do for Father's Day

A Cheer: (all youth and teens up front for the cheer)

F- Firm Hand of God
A- Admiration of God
T- Tender Mercies of God
H- Honor of God
E- Ever Loving Heart of God
R- Revelation of God

"Our Heavenly Father"

Characters

Cam
Daniel
Narrator 1
Narrator 2
Sis Tanisha
Sis Julia
Emily
Jessica

Narrator 1:   This play is about two families whose fathers are not currently living with their love ones. Cam and Jessica have no father. They are raised in a single family. Daniel and Emily have a father but he is deployed; their father is a cop in the United States Army. Daniel and Cam become good friends. They are fifteen years old. Jessica is eight years old, and Emily is ten years old. At first Jessica does not like Emily because Jessica thinks she is stuck up. Later on they become good friends. All characters are Christians.

It is early June 2005, a hot summer day. Daniel and Emily just moved in the neighborhood with their mother, Sis Tanisha, and their father is deployed somewhere in the Middle East. Cam and Jessica's mother tell them about their new neighbors and bake chocolate chip cookies for Cam and Jessica to take over to them.

The setting— The children are over Daniel and Emily's house in the backyard talking and playing.

Daniel: I miss my dad and am tired of him always being away.

Cam: What do you mean?

Emily: (interrupts) Our father is deployed and a cop in the United States Army and always gone, that is what my brother means!

Jessica: What is this? Can't your brother speak for himself; he is the oldest, isn't he?

Emily: Yeah, but!

Jessica: But what, Miss knows it all?

Emily: What did I ever do to you, Jessica?

Cam: Okay, Jessica, I think you owe Emily an apology.

Daniel: Does Jessica not like my sister?

Cam: Man, she's just being a brat. Jessica, if you can't be nice to Emily, I will tell Mom and send you home this very moment.

Jessica: All right, Emily. I am sorry can we start over being friends?

Narrator 2: Jessica and Emily go into Emily's house to play. Cam and Daniel stay outside playing basketball.

Cam: Where were we? Oh, I know. You were complaining about your father never being home. At least you got a father in your life.

Daniel: Where is your father?

Cam: Dad—that is funny. Jessica and I do not have a father. Our father walked out on our mother when Jessica was just a newborn baby. I was a little brat myself. I hated him for a long time but since I have been going to church. I get saved and baptized last year and went to anger management classes. I do not hate him anymore but I realized it is his loss for not being a part of our lives. God's going to hold him accountable for not being here for us and I know one father that loves me no matter what.

Daniel: Yeah, man I know the Heavenly Father. Just sometimes I am mad with our Heavenly Father because he allows the military to send my father away all the time. Do not get me wrong; I love Jesus and all that but it hurts and is scary when my dad has to go.

Cam: I can't pretend to know your pain but I feel the hurt of not having a father around. Do you mind if we pray? My mother says for us to pray to the Lord; God does not like to see his children in pain.

Daniel: Yes, let's pray that God sends my father home for Father's Day and we are together as a family.

Cam: And I want to pray that wherever my father is, Lord, touch his heart in a mighty way so he might own up to his responsibility to us, preferably soon. (The Lord's Prayer Matthew 6:9-15)

Narrator 1:   It is Father's Day, and Daniel and Emily are excited because they are going to the airport to pick up their father. Cam and Jessica receive a phone call from their father and will see him next week with a supervised visit per the mother's request (Sis Julia). Daniel asked his mom if Cam and his sister could come with them to the airport for the celebration.

Sis Tanisha (Daniel and Emily's mom):   Come on, we have to leave now. What are you doing?

Daniel: Mom, can Cam and Jessica go with us to the airport?

Sis Tanisha: Yes, if it is all right with their mother.

Sis Julia (Cam and Jessica's mom):   Yes, my children can go. Let me know if they give you any trouble, Sis Tanisha.

Narrator 2:   As you can see, Our Heavenly Father does answers prayers; all you have to do is ask him.

Inspired by God's Word

Dear Heavenly Father,

Though I don't always understand your reasons sometimes,

I want to thank you for the time you allowed me to spend with your child you planted within me——-A Mother's Love

Our beloved was yours first and we thank you for the time you allowed our baby to grow inside of me. We will always cherish this gracious and precious gift. We know, we will see our little one again—A Family's Love

Dedicated to the memory of _____

Why Should I?

For Jesus Christ hasn't given up on me,
So tell me, dear, why should I give up on you?

For Jesus Christ sacrificed himself for me,
Despite all the wrong I have done.

So then I will live my life as Jesus Christ did,
With love, peace, harmony, respect, strength, and positive integrity.

For Jesus Christ hasn't given up on me,
So tell me again, dear, why should I give up on you?

For Jesus Christ has committed himself to me,
Never once breaking his commitment to me.

Can't say the same for myself!
So tell me again, why should I give up on you?
When Jesus Christ hasn't ever given up on me.

Why should I give up on our relationship?
When Jesus Christ has never given up on his relationship with me.

Can't say the same for myself?
So tell me, dear, why should I give up on you?

It's Not About Me

It's not about me,
It's about God Almighty.
It's not about me,
It's about Jesus Christ.
It's not about me,
It's about the Kingdom of God.
It's not about me
It's about serving God with all thy heart.
It's not about me,
It's about serving God's people.
It's not about me,
It's about being a servant to Christ Jesus.
It's not about me,
It's about living your life for Jesus Christ.
It's not about me,
It's about having faith in the Lord.
It's not about me,
It's about believing the Son of God shed his blood to save us from our sins.
It's not about me,
It's about Our Lord and Saviour, Jesus Christ.
It's not about me.
It's not about you.
It's not about us.
It's not about we.
It 's about the Son of God.
It's about keeping an individual relationship with God open.
It's about staying close to the Heavenly Father.
It's about trusting and being aligned with God's Plan on our lives.
It's about standing with good integrity with man to follow from generation to generation.
It's about being a mighty warrior for Christ Jesus.
It's about preparing and working until Jesus' Return.
Will you be Ready for his Return?

Grandmother's Love

A Grandmother's Love is like no other.
She sees you in ways no other can see.
A Grandmother's Love is genuine and pure.
In her eyes you can do no wrong.
A Grandmother's Love is a treasure never lost.
Although she may leave you in body, a part of her lies deep within you.
You just wait and see.
One day you're be thinking about a phrase or saying and you will
soon realize that's what Grandmother use to say.
A part of her will surely rub off on you.
A Grandmother's Love is like no other and it's truly never lost.

M - Manifestation of God as Husband and Wife

A - Approval of God as Husband and Wife

R - Relationship as One with God and each other

R - Receptiveness to God and each other

I - Intimacy with God and each other

A - Appreciation to God and each other

G - Giving of each other as Husband and Wife

E - Expectations of each other as Husband and Wife

Marriage is no honeymoon, as many couples may think going into one. It is all about commitment, devotion, endurance, maturity, communication, stability, compromises (except your faith in Jesus Christ; never compromise your faith), giving, selflessness, connecting as one.

Wives, submitting to your husband means to support him, encourage him, influence him to make the right decisions.

Husbands, cherish your wife, admire her, treat her like the jewel God intended her to be, respect and honor her for her knowledge and spiritual guidance.
Proverbs 31:10 - 30

Marriage is hard work. Communication is the key. "Do not let your flames go completely out!"

Love never causes pain, and divorce should not be an easy way out. As a couple, you continue to learn to grow closer and closer as one. Each year should be richer than before.
Genesis 2:18 - 24 KJV

In Dedication of _____